THE SMASH BROADWAY COLLECTION

100 Great Songs of the Century

Project Manager: Sy Feldman
Production Coordinator: Donna Salzburg
Art Design: Jorge Paredes
Cast Photos: Photofest (unless otherwise indicated)

THE SMASH BROADWAY COLLECTION
CONTENTS

Title	Show	Pg. No.

Title	Show	Pg. No.

FUNNY FACE

L to R: Betty Compton, Adele Astaire, Gertrude McDonald, Fred Astaire

Song Highlights:
The Babbitt And The Bromide; Funny Face;
He Loves And She Loves; My One And Only
(What Am I Gonna Do); 'S Wonderful;
When The Right One Comes Along

Opened: 11/22/1927
Alvin Theatre
Broadway: 250 performances

Music: George Gershwin
Lyrics: Ira Gershwin
Book: Paul Gerard Smith, Fred Thompson
Producer: Alex A. Aarons, Vinton Freedley
Director: Edgar MacGregor
Choreographer: Bobby Connolly

Cast:
Adele Astaire, Fred Astaire, Betty Compton,
Allen Kearns, William Kent, Gertrude McDonald,
Victor Moore

Funny Face

HE LOVES AND SHE LOVES

Music and Lyrics by
GEORGE GERSHWIN
and IRA GERSHWIN

He Loves and She Loves - 4 - 1

8

two - some that just can't go wrong, hear me:

He loves and she loves and they love, So

won't you love me as I love
why can't you love me love and I love,
you. too?

He Loves and She Loves - 4 - 4

Showboat

BILL

Words by
P.G. WODEHOUSE
OSCAR HAMMERSTEIN II

Music by
JEROME KERN

Bill - 3 - 1

SHOW BOAT

L to R: Jan Clayton (Magnolia), Ethel Owen (Parthy),
Charles Fredericks (Gaylord Ravenal), Ralph Dumke (Capt. Andy)
1946 Revival

Opened: 12/27/1927
Ziegfeld Theatre
Broadway: 575 performances

Music: Jerome Kern
Lyrics: Oscar Hammerstein II
Book: Oscar Hammerstein II
Producer: Florenz Ziegfeld
Director: Zeke Colvan, Oscar Hammerstein II
Choreographer: Sammy Lee

Song Highlights:
Bill, Can't Help Lovin' Dat Man; Cotton Blossom;
Life Upon The Wicked Stage; Make Believe;
Ol' Man River; 'Till Good Luck Comes My Way;
Why Do I Love You?; You Are Love

Original Cast:
Jules Bledsoe, Tess Gardella, Francis X. Mahoney,
Howard Marsh, Helen Morgan, Edna May Oliver,
Eva Puck, Norma Terris, Sammy White,
Charles Winninger

Showboat

CAN'T HELP LOVIN' DAT MAN

Words by
OSCAR HAMMERSTEIN II

Music by
JEROME KERN

Showboat

MAKE BELIEVE

Words by
OSCAR HAMMERSTEIN II

Music by
JEROME KERN

The game of "just sup-pos-ing" is the sweet-est game I know,

Our dreams are more ro-man-tic than the world we see.

Make Believe - 4 - 1

And if the things we dream a-bout don't hap-pen_ to be so,_

That's just an un-im-por-tant tech-ni-cal-i-ty._

Refrain *At a slow even pace (expressively)*

We could make be-lieve _ I love you,_ On-ly make be-lieve_

_ that you love me. _ Oth-ers find peace of mind in pre-

Make Believe - 4 - 2

OL' MAN RIVER

Lyrics by
OSCAR HAMMERSTEIN II

Music by
JEROME KERN

Piano

Col - ored folks work on de Mis - sis - sip - pi, Col - ored folks work while de white folks play,

Pull - in' dose boats from de dawn to sun - set, Git - tin' no rest till de judge - ment day.

Ol' Man River - 5 - 2

don't plant cot-ton, An' dem dat plants 'em is soon for-got-ten; But

ol' man riv-er, he jus' keeps roll-in' a - long.

You an' me, we sweat an' strain,

Bod-y all ach-in' an' racked wid pain. "Tote dat barge!"

Ol' Man River - 5 - 4

NO, NO, NANETTE

Ruby Keeler, Bobby Van and Cast (1971 Revival)

Opened: 9/16/1925
Globe Theatre
Broadway: 329 performances

Music: Vincent Youmans
Lyrics: Irving Caesar
Book: Otto Harbach, Frank Mandel
Producer & Director: H.H. Frazee
Choreographer: Sammy Lee

Song Highlights:
I Want To Be Happy;
I've Confessed To The Breeze I Love You;
No, No, Nanette; Take A Little One Step;
Tea For Two; Too Many Rings Around Rosie

Original Cast:
Jack Barker, Wellington Cross, Elinor Dawn,
Louis Groody, Mary Lawlor, Beatrice Lee,
Georgia O'Ramey, Edna Whistler,
Josephine Whittell,
Charles Winninger

I WANT TO BE HAPPY

Words by
IRVING CAESAR

Music by
VINCENT YOUMANS

Moderato

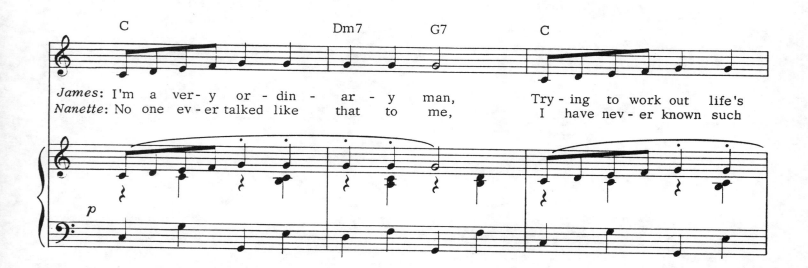

James: I'm a ver-y or-din-ar-y man,   Try-ing to work out life's
Nanette: No one ev-er talked like that to me,   I have nev-er known such

hap - py plan,   Do - ing un - to oth - ers as I'd
sym - pa - thy,   On - ly in my dreams, it real - ly

I Want to Be Happy - 4 - 1

Refrain

WHO?

Words by
OTTO HARBACH and
OSCAR HAMMERSTEIN II

Music by
JEROME KERN

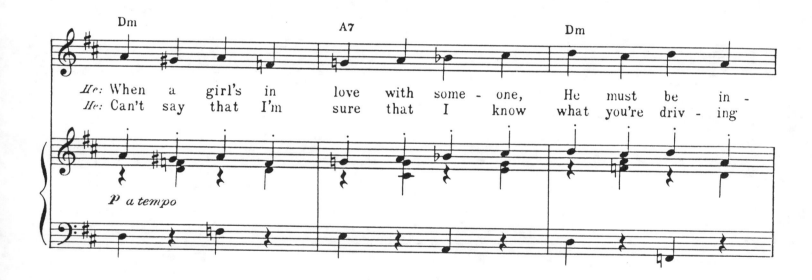

Who? - 4 - 1

She: Then if I'm in love with some-one,
She: Make your mind up, don't be shy, no

I must wait un - til there'll come one
game of ee - nie, mee - nie - mi - no

mask.
way.

Boy, who'll know the
Can be played with

an - swer when I ask:
la - dies when they say:

Refrain *(Smoothly)*

Who stole my heart

Who? - 4 - 4

SUNNY

L to R: Esther Howard, Joseph Cawthorn, Dorothy Francis, Clifton Webb,
Marilyn Miller, Paul Frawley, Mary Hay, Jack Donahue

Opened: 09/23/1925
New Amsterdam Theatre
Broadway: 517 performances

Music: Jerome Kern
Lyrics: Oscar Hammerstein II, Otto Harbach
Book: Oscar Hammerstein II, Otto Harbach
Producer: Charles Dillingham
Director: Hassard Short
Choreographer: Fred Astaire, David Bennett,
Alexis Kosloff, Julian Mitchell, John Tiller

Song Highlights:
Just A Little Thing Called Rhythm; Paddlin' Madelin'
Home; Sunny; Two Little Bluebirds; Who?

Cast:
Charles Angelo, Joseph Cawthorn,
Jack Donahue, Cliff Edwards, Dorothy Francis,
Paul Frawley, Helen Gardner, Mary Hay,
Esther Howard, Pert Kelton, Marilyn Miller,
Clifton Webb

Very Warm For May

ALL THE THINGS YOU ARE

Words by
OSCAR HAMMERSTEIN II

Music by
JEROME KERN

Moderato

Time and a-gain I've longed for ad-ven-ture, Some-thing to make my

heart beat the fast-er. What did I long for? I nev-er real-ly

knew.

Find-ing your love I've found my ad-ven-ture,

All the Things You Are - 4 - 1

All the Things You Are - 4 - 2

All the Things You Are - 4 - 3

GIRL CRAZY

Ginger Rogers

Opened: 10/14/1930
Alvin Theatre
Broadway: 272 performances

Music: George Gershwin
Lyrics: Ira Gershwin
Book: Guy Bolton, John McGowan
Producer: Alex A. Aarons, Vinton Freedley
Director: Alexander Leftwich
Choreographer: George Hale

Song Highlights:
Bidin' My Time; Boy! What Love Had Done To Me!;
But Not For Me; Could You Use Me?;
Embraceable You; I Got Rhythm; Treat Me Rough

Cast:
Antonio DeMarco, Renee DeMarco, Jimmy Dorsey,
Roger Edens, The Foursome, Benny Goodman,
Eunice Healey, Willie Howard, Allen Kearns,
William Kent, Gene Krupa, Ethel Merman,
Glenn Miller, Red Nichols Orchestra, Lew Parker,
Ginger Rogers, Jack Teagarden

Note: The orchestra included Benny Goodman,
Glenn Miller, Red Nichols, Jimmy Dorsey,
Jack Teagarden and Gene Krupa

Girl Crazy

BUT NOT FOR ME

Music and Lyrics by
GEORGE GERSHWIN
and IRA GERSHWIN

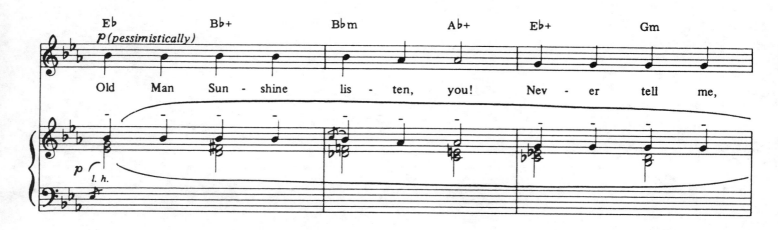

Old Man Sun - shine lis - ten, you! Nev - er tell me,

"Dreams come true!" Just try it And I'll start a ri - ot.

But Not for Me - 4 - 1

But Not for Me - 4 - 2

The Boys From Syracuse

FALLING IN LOVE WITH LOVE

Words by
LORENZ HART

Music by
RICHARD RODGERS

Falling in Love With Love - 6 - 1

Falling in Love With Love - 6 - 5

I GET A KICK OUT OF YOU

Words and Music by
COLE PORTER

I Get a Kick Out of You - 4 - 1

REFRAIN

I Get a Kick Out of You - 4 - 2

I Get a Kick Out of You - 4 - 4

I WISH I WERE IN LOVE AGAIN

Words by
LORENZ HART

Music by
RICHARD RODGERS

I Wish I Were in Love Again - 4 - 1

58

I Wish I Were in Love Again - 4 - 4

Babes In Arms

MY FUNNY VALENTINE

Words by
LORENZ HART

Music by
RICHARD RODGERS

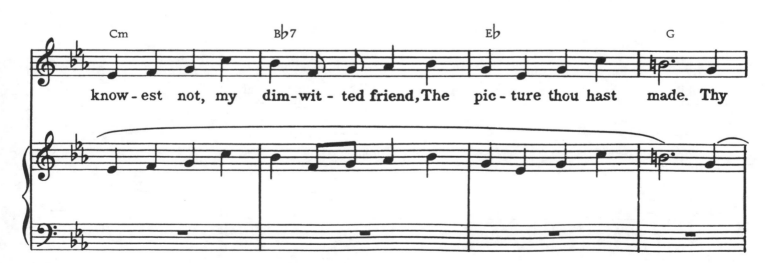

My Funny Valentine - 4 - 1

Roberta

SMOKE GETS IN YOUR EYES

Words by
OTTO HARBACH

Music by
JEROME KERN

Cast on Catfish Row

Opened: 10/10/1935
Alvin Theatre
Broadway: 124 performances

Music: George Gershwin
Lyrics: Ira Gershwin, DuBose Heyward
Book: DuBose Heyward
Producer: The Theatre Guild
Director: Rouben Mamoulian

Song Highlights:
Bess, You Is My Woman Now;
I Got Plenty O' Nuttin'; I Loves You, Porgy;
I'm On My Way; It Ain't Necessarily So;
My Man's Gone Now; Summertime;
There's A Boat Dat's Leavin' Soon For New York;
Woman Is A Sometime Thing

Cast:
Anne Brown, John Bubbles, Ford Buck,
Warren Coleman, Helen Dowdy, Todd Duncan,
Ruby Elzy, Georgette Harvey, J. Rosamond Johnson,
Edward Matthews, Abbie Mitchell, Musa Williams

Porgy and Bess

SUMMERTIME

By
GEORGE GERSHWIN,
DU BOSE and DOROTHY HEYWARD
and IRA GERSHWIN

Summertime - 4 - 1

morn-in'_____ there's a noth-in' can harm you_____

With Dad-dy an' Mam-my stand-in'

by._____

OF THEE I SING

L to R: William Gaxton, Lois Moran, George Murphy, Victor Moore

Opened: 12/26/1931
Music Box Theatre
Broadway: 446 performances

Music: George Gershwin
Lyrics: Ira Gershwin
Book: George S. Kaufman, Morrie Ryskind
Producer: Sam H. Harris
Director: George S. Kaufman
Choreographer: George Hale

Song Highlights:
Because, Because; The Illegitimate Daughter;
A Kiss For Cinderella; Love Is Sweeping The Country;
Of Thee I Sing; Who Cares?;
Wintergreen For President

Cast:
Florenz Ames, Grace Brinkley, Dudley Clements,
William Gaxton, George E. Mack, Sam Mann,
Harold Moffatt, Victor Moore, Lois Moran,
George Murphy, James O'Dea, Ralph Riggs,
Edward H. Robins

Of Thee I Sing

WHO CARES?

Music and Lyrics by
GEORGE GERSHWIN
and IRA GERSHWIN

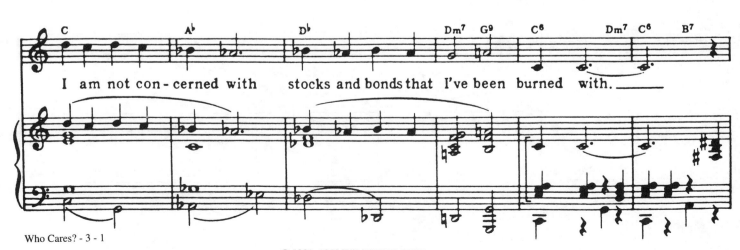

Who Cares? - 3 - 1

74

Who Cares? - 3 - 2

PAL JOEY

Vivienne Segal and Gene Kelly

Opened: 12/15/1940
Ethel Barrymore Theatre
Broadway: 374 performances

Music: Richard Rodgers
Lyrics: Lorenz Hart
Book: George Abbott, John O'Hara
Producer & Director: George Abbott
Choreographer: Robert Alton

Song Highlights:
Bewitched, Bothered And Bewildered;
Do It The Hard Way; I Could Write A Book;
Plant You Now, Dig You Later; Take Him;
You Musn't Kick It Around; Zip

Cast:
Jean Casto, Stanley Donen, Jack Durant,
Leila Ernst, Jane Fraser, June Havoc, Van Johnson,
Gene Kelly, Robert J. Mulligan, Vivienne Segal

Pal Joey

BEWITCHED

Words by
LORENZ HART

Music by
RICHARD RODGERS

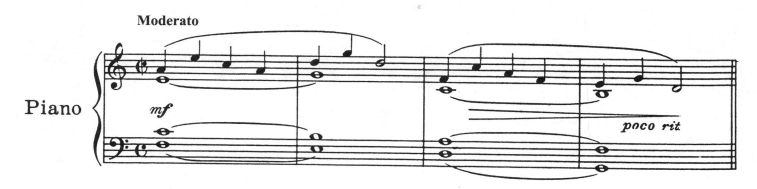

He's a fool and don't I know it, But a fool can have his charms;

I'm in love and don't I show it, Like a babe in arms.

Bewitched - 4 - 1

BRIGADOON

James Mitchell (first row center) and Cast

Opened: 03/13/1947
Ziegfeld Theatre
Broadway: 581 performances

Music: Frederick Lowe
Lyrics: Alan Jay Lerner
Book: Alan Jay Lerner
Producer: Cheryl Crawford
Director: Robert Lewis
Choreographer: Agnes de Mille

Song Highlights:
Almost Like Being In Love; Come To Me;
Bend To Me; The Heather On The Hill;
I'll Go Home With Bonnie Jean;
There But For You Go I;
Waitin' For My Dearie

Cast:
Marion Bell, Pamela Britton, David Brooks,
Helen Gallagher, George Keane, James Mitchell,
Lee Sullivan

Brigadoon

ALMOST LIKE BEING IN LOVE

Lyrics by
ALAN JAY LERNER

Music by
FREDERICK LOEWE

Almost Like Being in Love - 2 - 1

ON THE TOWN

Chris Alexander and Nancy Walker

Opened: 12/28/1944
Adelphi Theatre
Broadway: 462 performances

Music: Leonard Bernstein
Lyrics: Betty Comden, Adolph Green
Book: Betty Comden, Adolph Green
Producer: Paul Feigay, Oliver Smith
Director: George Abbott
Choreographer: Jerome Robbins

Song Highlights:
Carried Away; I Can Cook Too; Lonely Town;
Lucky To Be Me; New York, New York; Ya Got Me

Cast:
Chris Alexander, John Battles, Betty Comden,
Adolph Green, Ray Harrison, Sono Osato,
Alice Pearce, Nancy Walker

On The Town

LUCKY TO BE ME

Words by
BETTY COMDEN and ADOLPH GREEN

Music by
LEONARD BERNSTEIN

Lucky to Be Me - 4 - 1

now that I've found you I've changed my point of view; And now I would-n't give a

dime to be an-y-one else but me.

ritard. _ _ _ _ a tempo

REFRAIN

What a day, for-tune smiled and came my way, bring-ing love I

mp-mf legato

nev-er thought I'd see, I'm so LUCK-Y TO BE ME;

The Threepenny Opera

English Words by
MARC BLITZSTEIN
Original German Words by
BERT BRECHT

MACK THE KNIFE

Music by
KURT WEILL

Moderate, with beat

Oh, the shark has ____ pret-ty teeth, dear ____ And he shows them ____ pearl-y white. ____

____ Just a jack-knife ____ has Mac-heath, dear ____ And he keeps it ____ out of sight. ____ When the shark bites ____ with his teeth, dear ____ Scar-let

Mack the Knife - 3 - 1

Mack the Knife - 3 - 3

THE THREEPENNY OPERA

Scott Merrill (Macheath) and Lotte Lenya (Jenny) from
the 1954 New York production of *The Threepenny Opera*

Opened: 03/10/1954
Theatre de Lys
Off-Broadway: 2,705 performances

Music: Kurt Weill
Lyrics: Marc Blitzstein
Based on original German lyrics by Bertolt Brecht
Book: Marc Blitzstein
Producer: Carmen Capalbo, Stanley Chase
Director: Carmen Capalbo

Songs:
Army Song; Ballad Of Mack The Knife; Love Song;
Pirate Jenny; Solomon Song

Cast:
Beatrice Arthur, John Astin, Joseph Beruh,
Bernard Bogin, Paul Dooley, Lotte Lenya,
Scott Merrill, Gerald Price, Charlotte Rae,
Jo Sullivan, George Tyne, Martin Wolfson

DAMN YANKEES

Stephen Douglass and Gwen Verdon

Opened: 05/05/1955
46th Street Theatre
Broadway: 1,019 performances

Music: Richard Adler, Jerry Ross
Lyrics: Richard Adler, Jerry Ross
Book: George Abbott, Douglass Wallop
Producer: Frederick Brisson, Robert E. Griffith, Harold Prince
Director: George Abbott
Choreographer: Bob Fosse

Song Highlights:
Goodbye, Old Girl; A Little Brains-A Little Talent;
Near You; Shoeless Joe From Hannibal Mo;
Those Were The Good Old Days; Two Lost Souls;
Whatever Lola Wants (Lola Gets);
You've Got To Have Heart

Cast:
Rae Allen, Shannon Bolin, Russ Brown,
Stephen Douglass, Nathaniel Frey, Jimmy Komack,
Eddie Phillips, Robert Shafer, Jean Stapleton,
Gwen Verdon, Ray Walston

HEART

Words and Music by
RICHARD ADLER
and JERRY ROSS

Moderate soft shoe tempo

You've got-ta have Heart, All you real-ly need is Heart,

When the odds are say-in' you'll nev-er win,— That's when the grin should start.

You've got-ta have hope, Must-n't sit a-round and mope,

Heart - 3 - 1

Noth-in's half as bad as it may ap-pear,— Wait-'ll next year and hope.

When your luck is bat-tin' ze-ro, — Get your chin up off the floor;

Mis-ter, you can be a he-ro, — You can o-pen an-y

door, there's noth-in' to it, but to do it, you've got-ta have Heart,

THE PAJAMA GAME

Janis Paige and John Raitt

Opened: 05/13/1954
St. James Theatre
Broadway: 1,061 performances

Music: Richard Adler, Jerry Ross
Lyrics: Richard Adler, Jerry Ross
Book: George Abbott, Richard Bissell
Producer: Frederick Brisson,
Robert E. Griffith,
Harold Prince
Director: George Abbott, Jerome Robbins
Choreographer: Bob Fosse

Song Highlights:
Hernando's Hideaway; Hey There;
I'm Not At All In Love; Once A Year Day;
The Pajama Game; 7 1/2 Cents; Steam Heat;
Racing With The Clock

Cast:
Marion Colby, Ralph Dunn, Eddie Foy Jr.,
Peter Gennaro, Carol Haney, Buzz Miller, Janis Paige,
Thelma Pelish, Stanley Prager, John Raitt,
Reta Shaw, Jack Waldron

STEAM HEAT

Words and Music by
RICHARD ADLER
and JERRY ROSS

*Symbols for Guitar, Diagrams for Ukulele

Steam Heat - 4 - 1

(clang) (clang) S- S- S- Steam Heat__ But I can't get warm with-out your hand to hold. The

ra- di- a- tor's hiss- in', Still I need your kiss- in' to keep me from freez- in' each

night! I got a hot wat-er bot-tle but noth-ing I got-'ll take the

place of you__ hold-ing me tight. I got (clang) (clang) S- S- S- Steam Heat.__ I got

Bye Bye Birdie

PUT ON A HAPPY FACE

Lyrics by
LEE ADAMS

Music by
CHARLES STROUSE

Rhythmically *(lightly)*

Refrain

Gray skies are gon-na clear up,_____ PUT ON A HAP-PY FACE;

Brush off the clouds and cheer up,_____ PUT ON A HAP-PY FACE.

Take off the gloom-y mask of trag-e-dy, It's not your style;

Put on a Happy Face - 2 - 1

BYE BYE BIRDIE

Dick Van Dyke and Chita Rivera

Opened: 04/14/1960
Martin Beck Theatre
Broadway: 607 performances

Music: Charles Strouse
Lyrics: Lee Adams
Book: Michael Stewart
Producer: L. Slade Brown, Edward Padula
Director: Gower Champion
Choreographer: Gower Champion

Song Highlights:
Hymn For A Sunday Evening; Kids;
A Lot Of Livin' To Do; One Boy (One Girl);
One Last Kiss; Put On A Happy Face

Cast:
Dick Gautier, Paul Lynde, Marijane Maricle,
Kay Medford, Michael J. Pollard, Chita Rivera,
Dick Van Dyke, Susan Watson

Bye Bye Birdie

A LOT OF LIVIN' TO DO

Words by
LEE ADAMS

Music by
CHARLES STROUSE

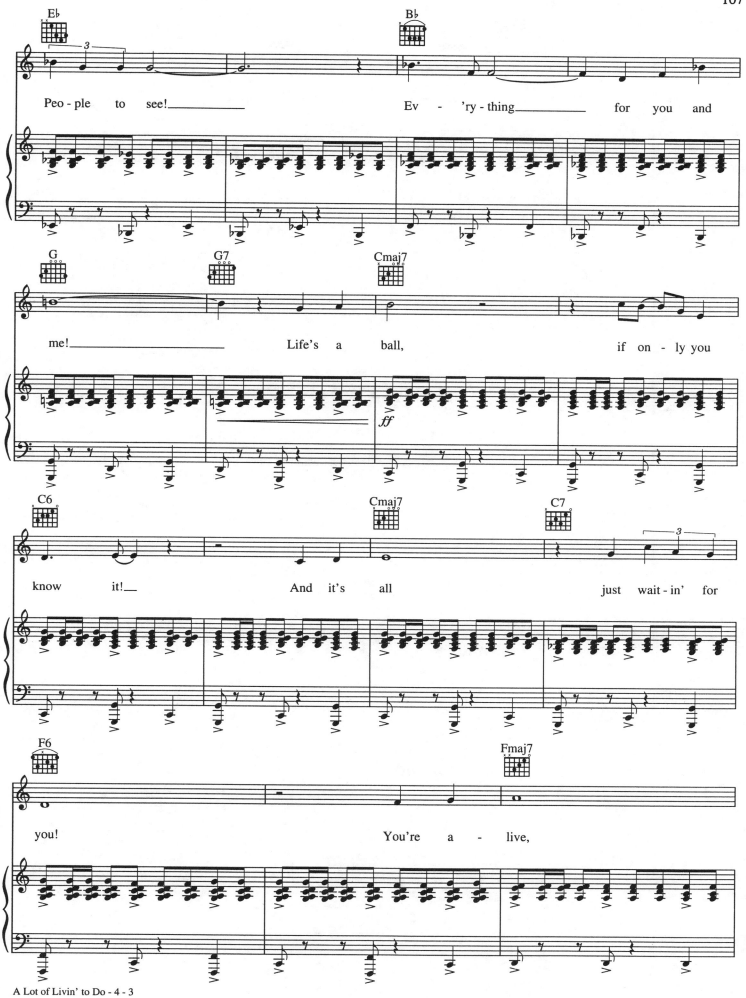

WILDCAT

Lucille Ball (and friend)

Lucille Ball and Keith Andes
(with Valerie Harper to right of Andes)

Opened: 12/16/1960
Alvin Theatre
Broadway: 171 performances

Music: Cy Coleman
Lyrics: Carolyn Leigh
Book: N. Richard Nash
Producer: Michael Kidd, N. Richard Nash
Director: Michael Kidd
Choreographer: Michael Kidd

Song Highlights:
Give A Little Whistle (And I'll Be There);
Hey, Look Me Over; I Hear (Oil); Tippy Tippy Toes;
What Takes My Fancy; You've Come Home

Cast:
Keith Andes, Lucille Ball, Clifford David, Edith King,
Al Lanti, Paula Stewart, Swen Swenson, Don Tomkins

Wildcat

HEY, LOOK ME OVER

Music by
CY COLEMAN

Lyrics by
CAROLYN LEIGH

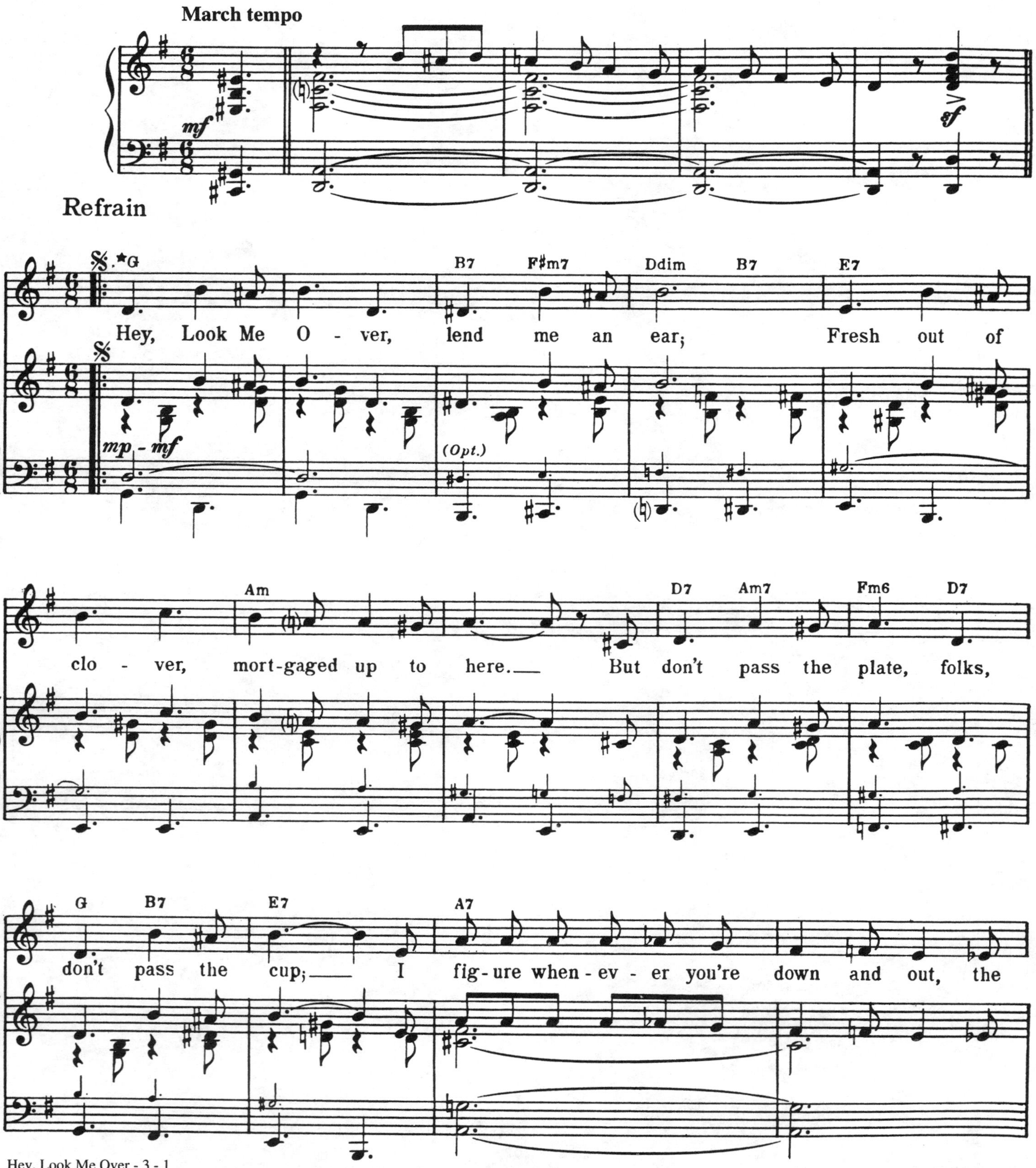
March tempo
mf
sf
Refrain
G
B7 F#m7 Ddim B7 E7
Hey, Look Me O - ver, lend me an ear; Fresh out of
mp - mf
(Opt.)
Am D7 Am7 Fm6 D7
clo - ver, mort-gaged up to here. But don't pass the plate, folks,
G B7 E7 A7
don't pass the cup; I fig-ure when-ev - er you're down and out, the

Hey, Look Me Over - 3 - 2

Interlude (*ad lib.*)

No - bod - y in the world was ev - er with - out a pray'r;

How can you win the world, if no - bod - y knows you're there.

Kid, when you need the crowd, the tick - ets are hard to sell;

Still you can lead the crowd, if you can get up and yell:

Tenderloin

ARTIFICIAL FLOWERS

Lyrics by
SHELDON HARNICK

Music by
JERRY BOCK

Artificial Flowers - 3 - 1

*pronounced like "wine"

LOVE MAKES THE WORLD GO 'ROUND

Words and Music by
BOB MERRILL

Love Makes the World Go 'Round - 2 - 1

HER FACE

Words and Music by
BOB MERRILL

Her Face - 3 - 1

Meas-ur-ing me, Star-ing at me, Meas-ur-ing me.

Refrain: Moderately (*with feeling*)

Ev-'ry-where I look I can see HER FACE _____ I can

see HER·FACE; See it ev-'ry-where. And

when I close my eyes it stays _____ And

like a leaf, whirls on a wind; a-round my mind it plays. If in

cresc. poco a poco

Her Face - 3 - 2

LITTLE ME

Sid Caesar

Opened: 11/17/1962
Lunt-Fontanne Theatre
Broadway: 257 performances

Music: Cy Coleman
Lyrics: Carolyn Leigh
Book: Neil Simon
Producer: Cy Feuer, Ernest Martin
Director: Cy Feuer, Bob Fosse
Choreographer: Bob Fosse

Song Highlights:
Be A Performer!; Boom-Boom
(Le Grand Boom-Boom);
Here's To Us; I've Got Your Number;
The Other Side Of The Tracks; Real Live Girl

Cast:
John Anania, Nancy Andrews, Sid Caesar,
Gretchen Cryer, Mickey Deems, Joey Faye,
Eddie Gasper, Marc Jordan, Mort Marshall,
Virginia Martin, Adnia Rice, John Sharpe,
Michael Smuin, Swen Swenson, Peter Turgeon

REAL LIVE GIRL

Music by
CY COLEMAN

Lyrics by
CAROLYN LEIGH

123

Real Live Girl - 2 - 2

Fiorello!

'TIL TOMORROW

Lyrics by
SHELDON HARNICK

Music by
JERRY BOCK

Twi - light de - scends; ev' - ry - thing ends 'TIL TO - MOR -

ROW,_____ to - mor - row. Since we must part,

'Til Tomorrow - 2 - 1

Fiorello!

LITTLE TIN BOX

Lyrics by
SHELDON HARNICK

Music by
JERRY BOCK

Allegretto con brio

(spoken)
1st time: First witness!
2nd time: Next witness!
3rd time: Next witness, take the stand.

1. Mis-ter "X", may we ask you a ques - tion? It's a - maz - ing, is it not, that the cit - y pays you slight-ly less than fif - ty bucks a week, yet you've pur-chased a pri - vate

2. Mis-ter "Y", we've been told you don't feel well and we know you've lost your voice, but we won-dered how you man-aged on the sal - a - ry you make to ac-qui - re a new Rolls

3. Mis-ter "Z", you're a jun - ior of - fi - cial and your in - come's rath - er low, yet you've kept a doz - en wom-en in the ver - y best ho - tels. Would you kind - ly ex - plain how

Little Tin Box - 4 - 1

ONCE UPON A TIME

Lyrics by
LEE ADAMS

Music by
CHARLES STROUSE

ONCE UP-ON A TIME a girl with moon-light in her eyes

Put her hand in mine and said she loved me

so. But that was ONCE UP-ON A TIME, ver-y long a-

WALKING HAPPY

Words by
SAMMY CAHN

Music by
JAMES VAN HEUSEN

SHE LOVES ME

Lyric by
SHELDON HARNICK

Music by
JERRY BOCK

She Loves Me - 4 - 2

She Loves Me - 4 - 4

A ROOM WITHOUT WINDOWS

Words and Music by
ERVIN DRAKE

A Room Without Windows - 4 - 1

Golden Boy

THIS IS THE LIFE

Lyrics by
LEE ADAMS

Music by
CHARLES STROUSE

This Is___ The Life! Here's where___ the liv-in' is!
This Is___ The Life! Here's where___ it's hap-pen-ing!

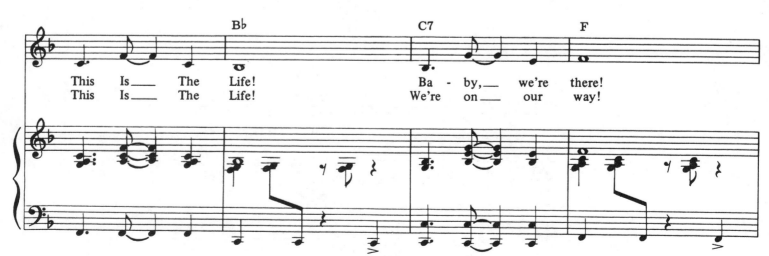

This Is___ The Life! Ba-by,___ we're there!
This Is___ The Life! We're on___ our way!

This Is the Life - 3 - 1

148

This Is the Life - 3 - 3

FIDDLER ON THE ROOF

Zero Mostel (left) singing "To Life"

Opened: 09/22/1964
Imperial Theatre
Broadway: 3,242 performances

Music: Jerry Bock
Lyrics: Sheldon Harnick
Book: Joseph Stein
Producer: Harold Prince
Director: Jerome Robbins
Choreographer: Jerome Robbins

Song Highlights:
Far From The Home I Love; If I Were A Rich Man;
Matchmaker, Matchmaker; Miracle Of Miracles;
Sunrise, Sunset; To Life; Tradition

Cast:
Beatrice Arthur, Bert Convy, Tanya Everett,
Michael Granger, Maria Karnilova, Joanna Merlin,
Julia Migenes, Zero Mostel, Austin Pendleton,
Joe Ponazecki

IF I WERE A RICH MAN

Lyrics by
SHELDON HARNICK

Music by
JERRY BOCK

155

If I Were a Rich Man - 8 - 6

Fiddler On The Roof

SUNRISE, SUNSET

Lyrics by
SHELDON HARNICK

Music by
JERRY BOCK

Moderately slow waltz tempo *(soulful and wistful)*

1. Is this the lit-tle girl I car - ried?
2. Now is the lit-tle boy a bride - groom,

Is this the lit-tle boy at play?
Now is the lit-tle girl a bride.

I don't re-
Un - der the

mem-ber grow - ing old - er,
can - o - py I see

When
them, Side

did
by

Sunrise, Sunset - 4 - 1

Sunrise, Sunset - 4 - 2

Sunrise, Sunset - 4 - 4

Fiddler On The Roof

TO LIFE

Lyrics by
SHELDON HARNICK

Music by
JERRY BOCK

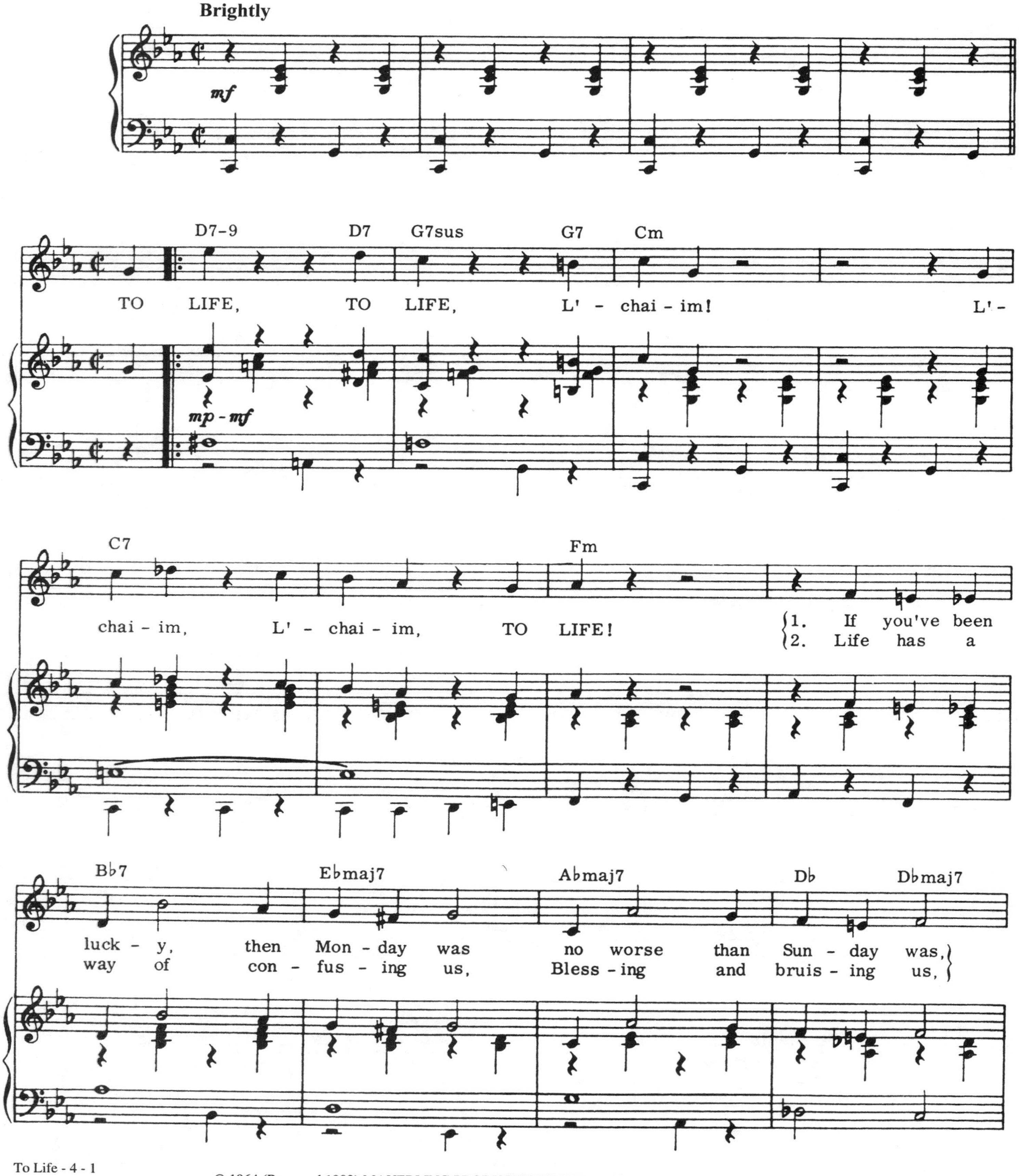

Brightly

TO LIFE, TO LIFE, L'-chai-im! L'-

chai-im, L'-chai-im, TO LIFE!

1. If you've been
2. Life has a

luck-y, then Mon-day was no worse than Sun-day was,
way of con-fus-ing us, Bless-ing and bruis-ing us,

To Life - 4 - 1

On A Clear Day You Can See Forever

COME BACK TO ME

Lyrics by
ALAN JAY LERNER

Music by
BURTON LANE

Come Back to Me - 5 - 1

ON A CLEAR DAY
(You Can See Forever)

Lyrics by
ALAN JAY LERNER

Music by
BURTON LANE

On a clear day ___ Rise and look a - round you ___

And you'll see who ___ you are. ___

On a clear day ___ How it will as - tound you ___

On a Clear Day - 3 - 1

On a Clear Day - 3 - 3

ON A CLEAR DAY YOU CAN SEE FOREVER

John Cullum and Barbara Harris

PROMISES, PROMISES

"Togetherness" is the theme of this dance number. Ted Pugh as C.C. Baxter is second from right.

Opened: 10/17/1965
Mark Hellinger Theatre
Broadway: 280 performances

Music: Burton Lane
Lyrics: Alan Jay Lerner
Book: Alan Jay Lerner
Producer: Alan Jay Lerner
Director: Robert Lewis
Choreographer: Herbert Ross

Song Highlights:
Come Back To Me; Melinda;
On A Clear Day You Can See Forever;
What Did I Have That I Don't Have

Cast:
Rae Allen, John Cullum, William Daniels,
Clifford David, Barbara Harris, Michael Lewis,
Gerry Matthews, Titos Vandis, Byron Webster

Opened: 12/01/1968
Shubert Theatre
Broadway: 1,281 performances

Music: Burt Bacharach
Lyrics: Hal David
Book: Neil Simon
Producer: David Merrick
Director: Robert Moore
Choreographer: Michael Bennett

Song Highlights:
I'll Never Fall In Love Again; Promises, Promises;
She Likes Basketball; Whoever You Are (I Love You)

Original Cast:
Carole Bishop, Graciela Daniele, Robert Fitch,
A. Larry Haines, Ken Howard, Baayork Lee,
Donna McKechnie, Marian Mercer, Jill O'Hara,
Jerry Orbach, Paul Reed, Margo Sappington,
Michael Shawn, Norman Shelly, Millie Slavin,
Edward Winter

Promises, Promises

I'LL NEVER FALL IN LOVE AGAIN

Words by
HAL DAVID

Music by
BURT BACHARACH

I'll Never Fall in Love Again - 4 - 1

I'LL NEV-ER FALL IN LOVE A-GAIN.

1. What do you get when you kiss a {guy-/girl} You get e-nough germs to catch
2. What do you get when you give your heart, You get it all bro-ken up
optional: 3. What do you get when you need a {girl,-/guy,-} You get e-nough tears to fill

— pneu-mo-nia, Aft-er you do, she'll nev-er phone you;
— and bat-tered, That's what you get, a heart that's shat-tered;}
— an o-cean, That's what you get for your de-vo-tion,

I'LL NEV-ER FALL IN LOVE A - GAIN._____

I'll Never Fall in Love Again - 4 - 2

I'LL NEV-ER FALL IN LOVE A-GAIN. _

Don't tell me what it's all a-bout, _ 'Cause I've been there _ and I'm

glad I'm out; _____ Out of those chains, those chains that bind _ you, That is why I'm

here to re-mind you
here to re-mind you. What do you get when you fall in love, _ You

I'll Never Fall in Love Again - 4 - 3

on - ly get lies and pain__ and sor - row, So for at least un - til to - mor - row,

I'LL NEV - ER FALL IN LOVE A - GAIN, _____

Repeat these 4 bars last time

1. I'LL NEV - ER FALL IN LOVE A - GAIN.__

2. NEV - ER FALL IN LOVE A - GAIN. _____

ritard *a tempo*

I'll Never Fall in Love Again - 4 - 4

HAIR

Steve Curry (#59), Shelley Plimpton (on mattress)
and other cast members

Above: Emaretta Marks, Melba Moore, Lorri Davis
Below: Suzannah Norstrand, Diane Keaton,
Natalie Mosco

Opened: 10/17/1967
Biltmore Theatre
Broadway: 1,836 performances

Music: Galt MacDermot
Lyrics: James Rado, Gerome Ragni
Book: James Rado, Gerome Ragni
Producer: Michael Butler
Director: Tom O'Horgan
Choreographer: Julie Arenel

Song Highlights:
Aquarius; Let The Sunshine In; Easy To Be Hard;
Good Morning, Starshine; Hair

Cast:
Steve Curry, Ronald Dyson, Sally Eaton, Paul Jabara,
Diane Keaton, Lynn Kellogg, Melba Moore,
Shelley Plimpton, James Rado, Gerome Ragni,
Lamont Washington

Hair

AQUARIUS

Words by
JAMES RADO and
GEROME RAGNI

Music by
GALT MacDERMOT

When the moon _____ is in the sev - enth house, _____ and
Ju - pi - ter _____ a - ligns ___ with Mars, _____ Then
peace, _____ will guide ___ the ___ plan - ets, _____ And

Aquarius - 3 - 1

Hair

GOOD MORNING STARSHINE

Words by
JAMES RADO
and GEROME RAGNI

Music by
GALT MacDERMOT

Good Morn - ing Star - shine, The earth says "Hel - lo".

You twin - kle a - bove us, We twin - kle be - low.

Good Morn - ing Star - shine, You lead us a -

Good Morning Starshine - 3 - 1

Good Morning Starshine - 3 - 3

Hair

LET THE SUNSHINE IN

Words by
JAMES RADO and GEROME RAGNI

Music by
GALT MacDERMOT

Moderately

Lyrics (vocal line):

We starve, look at one an-oth-er short of breath, walk-ing proud-ly in our win-ter coats, Wear-ing smells from lab-'ra-tor-ies, fac-ing a dy-ing na-tion of mov-ing pa-per fan-ta-sy, Lis-t'ning for the new told lies with su-

Let the Sunshine In - 3 - 1

Let the Sunshine In - 3 - 2

Sweet Charity

BIG SPENDER

Music by
CY COLEMAN

Lyrics by
DOROTHY FIELDS

The min-ute you walked in the joint, I could see you were a man of dis-tinc-tion, A real Big Spend-er,___ good look-ing,___ so re-fined.___ Say, would-n't you like to know what's go-ing on in my mind? So let me get right to the point,

Big Spender - 3 - 1

191

Big Spender - 3 - 3

SWEET CHARITY

Dancehall girls sing "Big Spender"

John McMartin and Gwen Verdon

Opened: 01/29/1966
Palace Theatre
Broadway: 608 performances

Music: Cy Coleman
Lyrics: Dorothy Fields
Book: Neil Simon
Producer: Lawrence Carr,
Robert Fryer, Joseph P. Harris
Director: Bob Fosse
Choreographer: Bob Fosse

Song Highlights:
Baby, Dream Your Dream; Big Spender;
If My Friends Could See Me Now;
I'm A Brass Band; Rhythm Of Life;
There's Gotta Be Something Better Than This;
Where Am I Going?

Cast:
Ruth Buzzi, Helen Gallagher, James Luisi,
John McMartin, Thelma Oliver, Harold Pierson,
Barbara Sharma, Arnold Soboloff, Gwen Verdon,
John Wheeler

Sweet Charity

IF MY FRIENDS COULD SEE ME NOW!

Music by
CY COLEMAN

Lyrics by
DOROTHY FIELDS

To-night at eight you should-a seen

a chauf-feur pull up in a rent-ed lim-ou-sine!

My neigh-bors burned! They like to die! When I

tell them who is get-tin' in and go-in' out is I! 1. If they could

If My Friends Could See Me Now! - 3 - 1

Mr. Wonderful

MR. WONDERFUL

Words and Music by
JERRY BOCK, LARRY HOLOFCENER
and GEORGE DAVID WEISS

Slowly and expressively

Mr. Wonderful - 4 - 1

Mr. Wonderful - 4 - 2

It's A Bird...It's A Plane...It's Superman®

YOU'VE GOT POSSIBILITIES

Lyrics by
LEE ADAMS

Music by
CHARLES STROUSE

You've Got Possibilities - 4 - 1

I'VE GOTTA BE ME

Music and Lyrics by
WALTER MARKS

I've Gotta Be Me - 3 - 1

A LITTLE NIGHT MUSIC

Glynis Johns and Hermione Gingold

Opened: 02/25/1973
Shubert Theatre
Broadway: 601 performances

Music & Lyrics: Stephen Sondheim
Book: Hugh Wheeler
Producer: Ruth Mitchell, Harold Prince
Director: Harold Prince
Choreographer: Patricia Birch

Song Highlights:
Liaisons; Miller's Son; Remember?;
Send In The Clowns; A Weekend In The Country;
You Must Meet My Wife

Cast:
George Lee Andrews, D'Jamin Bartlett,
Len Cariou, Despo, Patricia Elliott, Beth Fowler,
Hermione Gingold, Laurence Guittard, Glynis Johns,
Judy Kahan, Mark Lambert, Barbara Lang,
Victoria Mallory, Sherry Mathis, Teri Ralston,
Gene Varrone

SEND IN THE CLOWNS

Music and Lyrics by
STEPHEN SONDHEIM

This arrangement includes Mr. Sondheim's revised lyrics for Barbra Streisand's recording.

Send in the Clowns - 3 - 1

AIN'T MISBEHAVIN'

Words by
ANDY RAZAF

Music by
THOMAS "FATS" WALLER
and HARRY BROOKS

Ain't Misbehavin' - 4 - 1

are worth wait - in' for, be - lieve me.

I don't stay out late, don't care to go, I'm home a - bout eight, just

me and my ra - di - o, Ain't Mis - be - hav - in', I'm sav - in' my love for

you.

ANNIE

Andrea McArdle as Annie and Reid Shelton as Daddy Warbucks

Opened: 04/21/1977
Alvin Theatre
Broadway: 2,377 performances

Music: Charles Strouse
Lyrics: Martin Charnin
Book: Thomas Meehan
Producer: Lewis Allen, Stephen R. Friedman, Irwin Meyer, Mike Nichols
Director: Martin Charnin
Choreographer: Peter Gennaro

Song Highlights:
Annie; I Think I'm Gonna Like It Here;
It's The Hard-Knock Life; N.Y.C.; Tomorrow;
You're Never Fully Dressed Without A Smile

Cast:
Laurie Beechman, Danielle Brisebois, Shelley Bruce,
Sandy Faison, Robert Fitch, Dorothy Loudon,
Andrea McArdle, Reid Shelton, Raymond Thorne

IT'S THE HARD-KNOCK LIFE

Lyrics by
MARTIN CHARNIN

Music by
CHARLES STROUSE

Moderately, with a tough edge

It's the hard - knock life for us! It's the hard - knock life for us!

'Stead - a treat - ed___ we get tricked, 'Stead - a kiss - es___ we get kicked,

It's the hard-knock___ life! Got no folks to speak of, so,___

It's the Hard-Knock Life - 4 - 1

It's the Hard-Knock Life - 4 - 4

Annie

TOMORROW

Lyric by
MARTIN CHARNIN

Music by
CHARLES STROUSE

day that's gray and lone-ly,___ I just stick__ out my chin and grin and

say:_____ Oh! The sun-'ll come out____ to-mor-row,

{So you} got to hang on till to-mor-row___ come what may! To-
{Oh! I}

(small notes are optional harmony)

mor-row, to-mor-row, I love ya to-mor-row, you're {al-ways} a day a-
{on-ly}

Don't Bother Me, I Can't Cope

THANK HEAVEN FOR YOU

Words and Music by
MICKI GRANT

1. When I'm wor-ried, just a smile from you is all I need,
2. (When I'm) tired you can touch my brow and I'm good as new,

When I'm fail-ing, just a word from you and
And when trou-bles mul-ti-ply, you make them

I'll suc-ceed.
seem so few.

When I don't have a cent to my
And some-how you make me be-

name,   I'm still   rich in - deed. _____ 'Cause I've got
lieve   there's ___   noth-ing I can't do. _____ }

you   and your love to guide me, You   to   lie be - side me, With -

out you ___   I don't know what   I'd   do, _____

Thank Heav - en   For   You. _____   2. When I'm

Be - fore you came a - long   ev - r'y - thing went wrong,   and it

Thank Heaven for You - 3 - 3

APPLAUSE

Lauren Bacall

Opened: 03/30/1970
Palace Theatre
Broadway: 896 performances

Music: Charles Strouse
Lyrics: Lee Adams
Book: Betty Comden, Adolph Green
Producer: Lawrence Kasha, Joseph Kipness
Director: Ron Field
Choreographer: Ron Field

Song Highlights:
Applause; But Alive; Fasten Your Seat Belts;
Welcome To The Theatre; Who's That Girl?

Cast:
Lauren Bacall, Len Cariou, Bonnie Franklin,
Penny Fuller, Brandon Maggart, Robert Mandan,
Lee Roy Reams, Ann Williams

APPLAUSE

Lyric by
LEE ADAMS

Music by
CHARLES STROUSE

With a rock beat

What is it that we're liv - ing for?

Ap - plause, Ap -plause!____   Noth - ing I know____

brings on the glow ____   like sweet ap- plause.____

Applause - 3 - 1

Life seems to swing,___ and you're the king___ of it all, 'cause,
Soon as you hear,___ that hap-py au - di - ence roar, 'cause,

you've had___ a taste of the sound___ that says love,

Ap - plause, Ap - plause, Ap - plause!

plause!

Fade out

Applause - 3 - 3

DON'T BOTHER ME, I CAN'T COPE

Words and Music by
MICKI GRANT

(Spoken) I lay back on my analyst's couch
And told him what's frustratin' me.
He said, "The trouble with you is you can't cope!"
Then he asked me for a fifty dollar fee.

I said, "Don't Bother Me, I Can't Cope.
Do you think that I'm paying you that kind of dough
For telling me something I already know?
That's why I'm here, fool, 'cause I Can't Cope!"

(Sung) She said don't

both - er her,___ She can't cope!

D.S. for Verses 2, 3, 4.
Al Coda after narration of Verse 4.

Additional Verses:

2. *(Spoken)* I jumped in a taxi at one a.m.
But the cat wouldn't start the meter.
I said, "Listen, fella, I'm goin' downtown."
He said, "I don't go there either."

I said, "Don't Bother Me, I Can't Cope!
That sign says you can't refuse a fare,
So you or that sign better take me somewhere,
Because it's one a.m. and I Can't Cope!"

(Sung) He said don't bother him, he can't cope.

3. *(Spoken)* You know, I asked my boss for a raise in pay,
And he said, "You should have asked me yesterday.
Wages were frozen today, you see,
So all I can give you is sympathy."

And I said, "Don't fool with me, man, I Can't Cope.
You mean I've got to wait till the big freeze thaws?
Well, guess who's coming to dinner because
When my stomach starts growling, I Can't Cope!"

(Sung) He said don't bother him, he can't cope.

4. *(Spoken)* Ralph Abernathy told Jesse Jackson,
"Operation Breadbasket's doing fine.
But naughty little Jesse Horner,
Go stand in the corner
Until you learn how to stay in line."

Jesse said, "Shhhiii! Now you know I Can't Cope!
I'm not hidin' my light under no bush,
I know you've got pull
But I'm gonna get push,

Because between Operation S.C.L.C.,
Operation S.N.C.C.,
Operation "NEGRO",
Operation N.A.A.C.P.,
Operation "CORE",
And operation Richard J. Daley —
I Can't Cope!

But. . .

(Sung) You gotta cope
I gotta cope
All God's chillun gotta cope!

DON'T CRY FOR ME ARGENTINA

Lyrics by
TIM RICE

Music by
ANDREW LLOYD WEBBER

But all you have to do is look at me to know that ev - 'ry -

word is true.___

Evita

ANOTHER SUITCASE IN ANOTHER HALL

Lyrics by
TIM RICE

Music by
ANDREW LLOYD WEBBER

MISTRESS

1. I don't ex-pect my love af-fairs— to
2.3. *See additional lyrics*

last   for long;   Nev-er fool my-self   that my dreams— will come true:

Be-ing used to trou-ble I an-ti-ci-pate it,— but all the same I hate it,

Another Suitcase in Another Hall - 3 - 1

Another Suitcase in Another Hall - 3 - 2

Additional Lyrics

2. Time and time again I've said that I don't care;
   That I'm immune to gloom, that I'm hard through and through:
   But every time it matters all my words desert me;
   So anyone can hurt me and they do.

   So what happens now? . . . . etc., as above.

3. Call in three months' time and I'll be fine I know;
   Well maybe not that fine, but I'll survive anyhow:
   I won't recall the names and places of this sad occasion;
   But that's no consolation, here and now.

   So what happens now? . . . . etc., as above.

Evita

ON THIS NIGHT OF A THOUSAND STARS

Lyrics by
TIM RICE

Music by
ANDREW LLOYD WEBBER

On This Night of a Thousand Stars - 3 - 1

EVITA

Mandy Patinkin as Ché Guevara

SWEENEY TODD, THE DEMON BARBER OF FLEET STREET

Angela Lansbury and Len Cariou

Opened: 09/25/1979
Broadway Theatre
Broadway: 1,568 performances

Music: Andrew Lloyd Webber
Lyrics: Tim Rice
Producer: Robert Stigwood
Director: Harold Prince
Choreographer: Larry Fuller

Song Highlights:
And The Money Kept Rollin In;
Another Suitcase In Another Hall;
Don't Cry For Me Argentina; High Flying Adored;
On This Night Of A Thousand Stars; Rainbow High

Cast:
Bob Gunton, Patti LuPone, Jane Ohringer,
Mandy Patinkin, Mark Syers

Opened: 03/01/1979
Uris Theatre
Broadway: 557 performances

Music & Lyrics: Stephen Sondheim
Book: Hugh Wheeler
Producer: Richard Barr, Robert Fryer, Mary Lea
Johnson, Martin Richards, Charles Woodward
Director: Harold Prince
Choreographer: Larry Fuller

Song Highlights:
Ballad Of Sweeney Todd; By The Sea; Johanna;
Not While I'm Around; Pretty Women

Cast:
Len Cariou, Victor Garber, Cris Groenendaal,
Ken Jennings, Betsy Joslyn, Angela Lansbury,
Merle Louis, Edmund Lyndeck, Robert Ousley,
Sarah Rice, Joaquin Romaguera, Jack Eric Williams

Sweeney Todd

NOT WHILE I'M AROUND

Music and Lyrics by
STEPHEN SONDHEIM

Not to wor-ry, Not to wor-ry, I may not be smart, but I ain't dumb. Let me do it, Put me to it, Show me some-thing I can o-ver-come. Not to wor-ry, chum.

Andante placido (♩ = 112)

Poco rubato

Noth-ing's gon-na harm you, Not while I'm a-round.

Not While I'm Around - 3 - 1

Noth-ing's gon - na harm you, no sir, Not while I'm a - round.

De - mons are prowl - ing ev - 'ry - where, Now - a - days.

I'll send 'em howl - ing, I don't care, I got ways.

No-one's gon-na hurt you, No-one's gon-na dare.

Not While I'm Around - 3 - 2

Not While I'm Around - 3 - 3

Sweeney Todd

PRETTY WOMEN

Music and Lyrics by
STEPHEN SONDHEIM

Pretty Women - 4 - 1

standing on the ___ stair, Some-thing in them ___ cheers the

air. ___ Pret - ty wom - en.... ___

sil - hou - ett - ed.... ___ stay with - in you, ___ glanc - ing...

Stay for - ev - er, ___ breath - ing light - ly.... ___ Pret - ty wom - en, ___

Pretty Women - 4 - 2

pret - ty wom - en!___ Blow - ing out their can - dles or

comb - ing out their hair, E - ven when they___

leave,___ they still ___ are there. They're

there. Ah, Pret - ty wom - en, at their mir - rors, in their gar - dens,

let - ter - writ - ing, flow - er - pick - ing, weath - er - watch - ing, How they make a

man sing! Proof of heav - en ___ as you're liv - ing, ___

cresc. *f*

Pret - ty wom - en! ___ Yes, pret - ty wom - en! ___ Here's to

pret - ty wom - en, pret - ty wom - en, pret - ty wom - en, Pret - ty wom - en! ___

ff *morendo*

BEAUTIFUL CITY

Words and Music by
STEPHEN SCHWARTZ

Come sing me sweet___ re - joic - ing.
We don't need al - a - bas - ter.

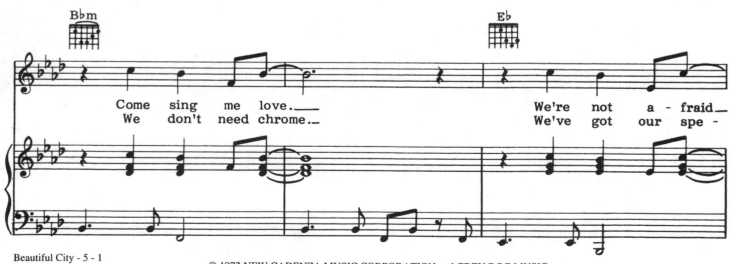

Come sing me love.___   We're not a - fraid___
We don't need chrome.___   We've got our spe -

Beautiful City - 5 - 1

On The Twentieth Century

OUR PRIVATE WORLD

Music by
CY COLEMAN

Lyrics by
BETTY COMDEN and ADOLPH GREEN

Moderately, with expression

we be - long _____ to - geth - er, You op - po - site me op - po - site you, Safe on our plan - et made on - ly for two. Night af - ter night, day af - ter day liv - ing our pri - vate two char - ac - ter play, Here in Our Pri - vate World. _____

TODAY IS THE FIRST DAY
OF THE REST OF MY LIFE

Lyrics by
RICHARD MALTBY, Jr.

Music by
DAVID SHIRE

Moderately, with suppressed excitment

Today Is the First Day of the Rest of My Life - 3 - 1

Today Is the First Day of the Rest of My Life - 3 - 3

JESUS CHRIST SUPERSTAR

Jeff Fenholt as Jesus, Marta Heflin as Mary Magdalene and Patrick Jude as Judas

Opened: 10/12/1971
Mark Hellinger Theatre
Broadway: 711 performances

Music: Andrew Lloyd Webber
Lyrics: Tim Rice
Producer: MCA, Robert Stigwood
Director: Tom O'Horgan

Song Highlights:
Heaven On Their Minds;
I Don't Know How To Love Him;
King Herod's Song; Superstar

Cast:
Paul Ainsley, Bob Bingham, Alan Braunstein,
Dennis Buckley, Barry Dennen, Yvonne Elliman,
Jeff Fenholt, Marta Heflin, Michael Jason, Phil Jethro,
Patrick Jude, Ben Vereen

I DON'T KNOW HOW TO LOVE HIM

Words by
TIM RICE

Music by
ANDREW LLOYD WEBBER

I Don't Know How to Love Him - 4 - 1

I Don't Know How to Love Him - 4 - 2

I Don't Know How to Love Him - 4 - 4

Jesus Christ Superstar

SUPERSTAR

Lyrics by
TIM RICE

Music by
ANDREW LLOYD WEBBER

Maestoso

Moderato (Freely — 'Soul' style)
(Voice of Judas)

C7   Eb   F7

Ev-'ry-time I look at you I don't un-der-stand __ Why you let the things you did get
Tell me what you think a-bout your friends at the top __ Who d'you think be-sides your-self's the

C7   Eb

so out of hand __ You'd have man-aged bet-ter if you'd had__ it planned__
pick of the crop? __ Bud-dah was he where it's at? Is he where you are? __

F7   C7

Why'd you choose such a back-ward time and such a strange land? __
Could Ma-hom-et__ move a moun-tain or was that just P R ?__

Superstar - 4 - 1

Your Arms Too Short To Box With God

WE'RE GONNA HAVE A GOOD TIME

Words and Music by
MICKI GRANT

We're Gonna Have a Good Time - 3 - 1

CORNER OF THE SKY

Words and Music by
STEPHEN SCHWARTZ

Corner of the Sky - 5 - 2

an - y - where I go?__
an - y - thing at all.__
- ter on__ the wind.

Riv - ers be - long__ where they can ram -

- ble, ____

Ea - gles be - long__ where they can fly;__

I've got to be__ where my

spir - it can run free,

Got to find my cor - ner __

Corner of the Sky - 5 - 3

of the sky.

Corner of the Sky - 5 - 5

THE WIZ

L to R: Stephanie Mills (Dorothy), Howard Porter (Tin Man),
Gregg Baker (Cowardly Lion), Charles Valentino (The Scarecrow)

Opened: 01/05/1975
Majestic Theatre
Broadway: 1,672 performances

Music & Lyrics: Charlie Smalls
Book: William F. Brown
Producer: Ken Harper
Director: Geoffrey Holder, Gilbert Moses
Choreographer: George Faison

Song Highlights:
Ease On Down The Road; Home;
If You Believe (Believe In Yourself);
No Bad News; What Would I Do If I Could Feel

Cast:
Hinton Battle, Danny Beard, Dee Dee Bridgewater,
Andre De Shields, Pi Douglass, Tiger Haynes,
Mabel King, Esther Marrow, Stephanie Mills,
Ted Ross, Clarice Taylor, Carl Earl Weaver,
Ralph Wilcox

HOME

Words and Music by
CHARLIE SMALLS

When I think of home, I think of a place where there's love o - ver -
May-be there's a chance for me to go back now that I have some di -

flow - ing. I wish I was home, I wish I was back there_ with the
rec - tion. It would sure be nice to be back_ home where there's

Home - 5 - 1

things I've been know-ing. Wind that makes the tall trees bend in-to lean-ing,
love and af-fec-tion. And just may-be I can con-vince time to slow up,

sud-den-ly the snow-flakes that fall have a mean-ing, sprink-ling____ the
giv-ing me e-nough time in my life to grow up. Time____ be my

scene makes it____ all clean.
friend, let me start a-gain.

The Wiz

BELIEVE IN YOURSELF

Words and Music by
CHARLIE SMALLS

If you be - lieve with-in your heart, you'll know that no - one can change the path that you must go. Be-lieve what you feel

THE GOLD DIGGERS' SONG

(We're in the Money)

Words by
AL DUBIN

Music by
HARRY WARREN

Gone are my blues, and gone are my tears; _____

I've got good news to shout in your ears. _____

The sil - ver dol - lar has re - turned to the fold, _____ with

The Gold Diggers' Song - 3 - 1

The Gold Diggers' Song - 3 - 2

42ND STREET

Lee Roy Reams and a bevy of beauties

Opened: 08/25/1980
Winter Garden Theatre
Broadway: 3,486 performances

Music: Harry Warren
Lyrics: Al Dubin
Book: Mark Bramble, Michael Stewart
Producer: David Merrick
Director: Gower Champion
Choreographer: Gower Champion

Song Highlights:
42nd Street; Lullaby Of Broadway; Shadow Waltz;
Shuffle Off To Buffalo; We're In The Money;
You're Getting To Be A Habit With Me

Cast:
Joseph Bova, Danny Carroll, Robert Colston,
Carole Cook, Don Crabtree, Tammy Grimes,
Jerry Orbach, Stan Page, Karen Prunczik,
Lee Roy Reams, Wanda Richert, Ron Schwinn

THINGS ARE LOOKING UP

Music and Lyrics by
GEORGE GERSHWIN
and IRA GERSHWIN

Things Are Looking Up - 3 - 1

Things Are Looking Up - 3 - 2

ONE NIGHT IN BANGKOK

By
BENNY ANDERSSON,
TIM RICE
and BJÖRN ULVAEUS

*Piano top line also vocal top line.

One Night in Bangkok - 7 - 3

One Night in Bangkok - 7 - 6

One Night in Bangkok - 7 - 7

NO ONE IS ALONE

Music and Lyrics by
STEPHEN SONDHEIM

No one here to guide you,___

Now you're on your own.___ On-ly me be-side you.___

___ Still you're not a-lone. No one is a-

No One Is Alone - 5 - 1

No One Is Alone - 5 - 2

Witch-es can be right, Gi-ants can be good, You de-cide what's

right, You de-cide what's good. Just re-mem-ber Some-one is on your side.

Some-one else is not. While you're see-ing your side,

May-be you for-got: They are not a-lone.

LITTLE SHOP OF HORRORS

Audrey II, the carnivorous plant from outer space

Opened: 07/27/1982
Orpheum Theatre
Broadway: 2,209 performances

Music: Alan Menken
Lyrics: Howard Ashman
Book: Howard Ashman
Producer: David Geffen, Cameron Mackintosh,
Shubert Organization, WPA Theatre
Director: Howard Ashman
Choreographer: Edie Cowan

Song Highlights:
Dentist!; Finale (Don't Feed The Plants);
Skid Row (Downtown); Somewhere That's Green;
Suddenly Seymour

Cast:
Hy Anzell, Marlene Danielle, Sheila Kay Davis,
Ellen Greene, Franc Luz, Martin P. Robinson,
Ron Taylor, Jennifer Leigh Warren, Lee Wilkof

SOMEWHERE THAT'S GREEN

Words by
HOWARD ASHMAN

Music by
ALAN MENKEN

Somewhere That's Green - 3 - 1

The Rink

MARRY ME

Lyrics by
FRED EBB

Music by
JOHN KANDER

Marry Me - 3 - 1

Merrily We Roll Along

GOOD THING GOING

Music and Lyrics by
STEPHEN SONDHEIM

Good Thing Going - 4 - 1

NOT A DAY GOES BY

Music and Lyrics by
STEPHEN SONDHEIM

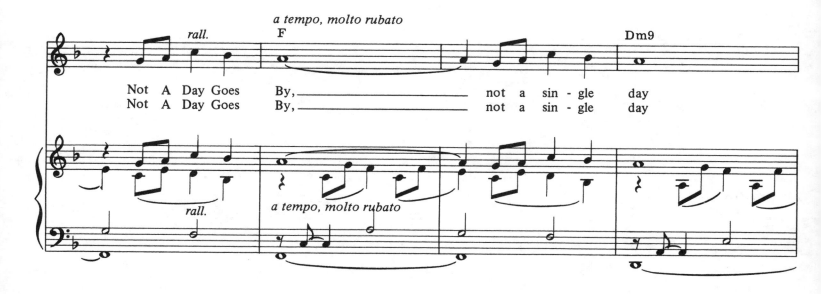

Not A Day Goes By,——————— not a sin-gle day
Not A Day Goes By,——————— not a sin-gle day

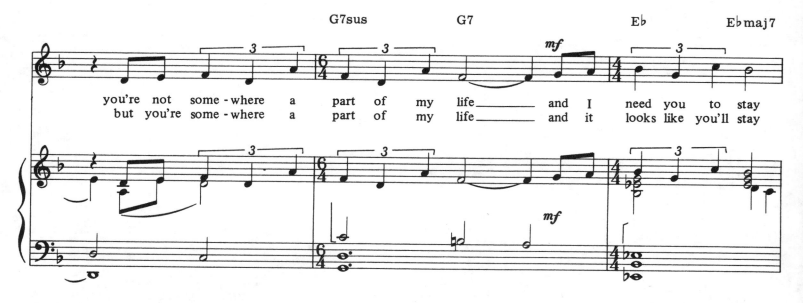

you're not some-where a part of my life——— and I need you to stay
but you're some-where a part of my life——— and it looks like you'll stay

Not a Day Goes By - 4 - 1

Not a Day Goes By - 4 - 4

SUNDAY IN THE PARK WITH GEORGE

Stars Bernadette Peters (center left) and Mandy Patinkin (center right)

Opened: 05/02/1984
Booth Theatre
Broadway: 604 performances

Music & Lyrics: Stephen Sondheim
Book: James Lapine
Producer: Emanuel Azenberg,
Playwrights Horizons, Shubert Organization
Director: James Lapine

Song Highlights:
Finishing The Hat; Move On; Putting It Together;
We Do Not Belong Together

Cast:
Barbara Byrne, Mary D'Arcy, Cris Groenendaal,
Dana Ivey, Charles Kimbrough, Nancy Opel,
Mandy Patinkin, Bernadette Peters,
Melanie Vaughan, Robert Westenberg

Sunday In The Park With George

PUTTING IT TOGETHER

Music and Lyrics by
STEPHEN SONDHEIM

Moderately fast (♩ = 126)

Bit by bit, Put-ting it to-geth-er.

Piece by piece. On-ly way to make a work of art.___ Ev-'ry mo-ment

makes a con-tri-bu-tion, Ev-'ry lit-tle de-tail plays a part.___ Hav-ing just the

Putting It Together - 12 - 1

324

Ev - 'ry min - or de - tail Is a maj - or de - ci - sion. Have to keep things in scale, Have to hold to your vi - sion -- What's a lit - tle cock - tail con - ver - sa - tion If __ it gets the funds for your found-a- __ tion? Ev - 'ry time I start to feel de - fen - sive, I __ re - mem-ber

332

Putting It Together - 12 - 10

do have the sus-pi - cion That it's tak-ing all your con - cen-tra - tion. The

art of mak - ing art _____ Is put-ting it to-

geth-er Bit by bit, Beat by

beat, Part by part, Sheet by sheet, Chart by chart, Track by

track, Reel by reel, Stack by stack, Deal by deal, Spat by

spat, Spiel by spiel, And that _____

Is the state of the art! _____

(sustain each note)

Sophisticated Ladies

DON'T GET AROUND MUCH ANYMORE

Words by
BOB RUSSELL

Music by
DUKE ELLINGTON

When I'm not play-ing sol-i-taire— I take a book down from the

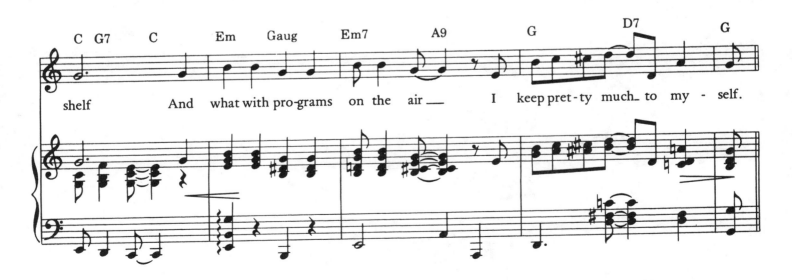

shelf   And what with pro-grams on the air— I keep pret-ty much— to my-self.

Don't Get Around Much Anymore - 3 - 1

Slowly

Missed the Sat-ur-day dance Heard they crowd-ed the floor

Could-n't bear it with-out ___ you ___ Don't get a-round much an-y - more.

Thought I'd vis-it the club Got as far as the door

They'd have asked me a-bout ___ you _ Don't get a-round much an-y - more. ___

Don't Get Around Much Anymore - 3 - 3

Sophisticated Ladies

IT DON'T MEAN A THING
(If It Ain't Got That Swing)

Words by
IRVING MILLS

Music by
DUKE ELLINGTON

It Don't Mean a Thing - 3 - 1

And The World Goes 'Round

BUT THE WORLD GOES 'ROUND

Lyrics by
FRED EBB

Music by
JOHN KANDER

But the World Goes 'Round - 5 - 1

WOMAN OF THE YEAR

Harry Guardino and Lauren Bacall

Opened: 03/29/1981
Palace Theatre
Broadway: 770 performances

Music: John Kander
Lyrics: Fred Ebb
Book: Peter Stone
Producer: Lawrence Kasha, David S. Landay,
Stewart F. Lane, James M. Nederlander,
Carole J. Shorenstein, Warner Theatre Productions
Director: Robert Moore
Choreographer: Tony Charmoli

Song Highlights:
The Grass Is Always Greener; I Wrote The Book;
One Of The Boys; See You In The Funny Papers;
Sometimes A Day Goes By

Cast:
Lauren Bacall, Helon Blount, Roderick Cook,
Marilyn Cooper, Harry Guardino, Rex Everhart,
Grace Keagy, Jamie Ross

Woman Of The Year

SOMETIMES A DAY GOES BY

Lyrics by
FRED EBB

Music by
JOHN KANDER

Flowingly, with expression

Some-times A Day Goes By, One whole en-tire day____ when

I_____ don't think of her._____

Twen-ty - four hours____ pass,____ I look a-round____ and find____ that

Sometimes a Day Goes By - 3 - 3

Beauty And The Beast

BE OUR GUEST

Words by
HOWARD ASHMAN

Music by
ALAN MENKEN

Lumiere: Ma chere Mademoiselle, it is with deepest pride and

greatest pleasure that we welcome you tonight. And now, we invite you to relax. Let us pull

up a chair as the dining room proudly presents - your dinner! Be our

Be Our Guest - 10 - 1

BEAUTY AND THE BEAST

Lyrics by
HOWARD ASHMAN

Music by
ALAN MENKEN

Female: Tale as old as____ time, Male: song as old as____ rhyme. Both: Beau-ty and the____

Beast.

rit.

mp

Freely

Beau-ty and the Beast.____

rit.

Beauty and the Beast - 6 - 6

Big

STARS, STARS, STARS

Lyrics by
RICHARD MALTBY, Jr.

Music by
DAVID SHIRE

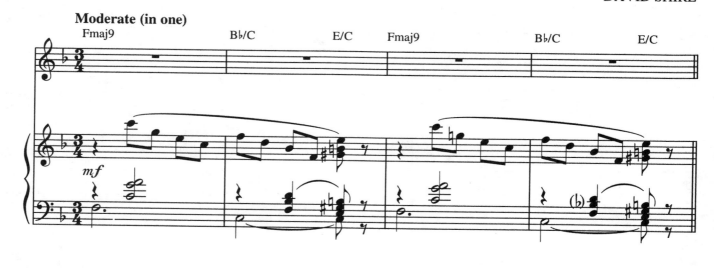

Stars, Stars, Stars - 3 - 1

Kiss Of The Spider Woman

THE KISS OF THE SPIDER WOMAN

Lyrics by
FRED EBB

Music by
JOHN KANDER

SPIDER WOMAN

Soon - er or la - ter you're cer - tain to meet in the bed - room, the
Soon - er or la - ter your love will ar - rive and he touch - es your

par - lor or e - ven the street. There's no place on earth you're
heart. You're a - lert and a - live and there's on - ly one pin that can

Kiss of the Spider Woman - 5 - 1

370

like - ly to miss | her kiss._____
punc - ture such bliss — | her kiss._____

Soon - er or la - ter in
Soon - er or la - ter you

sun - light or gloom when the red can - dles flick - er she'll walk in the
bathe in suc - cess and your min - ions sa - lute. They say no - thing but

room and the cur - tain will shake and the fi - re will hiss.
"yes" But your pow - er is emp - ty. It fades like the mist

Kiss of the Spider Woman - 5 - 2

Kiss of the Spider Woman - 5 - 3

SPIDER WOMAN

Chita Rivera

VICTOR/VICTORIA

Photo credit: Carol Rosegg/Joan Marcus/Photofest

Julie Andrews

Opened: 05/03/1993
Broadhurst Theatre
Broadway: 906 performances

Music: John Kander
Lyrics: Fred Ebb
Book: Terrence McNally
Producer: Livent, (U.S.) Inc.
Director: Harold Prince
Choreographer: Rob Marshall, Vincent Paterson

Song Highlights:
The Day After That; Dear One;
Kiss Of The Spider Woman; Only In The Movies;
Where You Are

Cast:
Kirsti Carnahan, Brent Carver, Anthony Crivello,
Philip Hernandez, Herndon Lackey, Merle Louis,
Michael McCormick, Chita Rivera

Opened: 10/25/1995
Marquis Theatre
Broadway: 738 performances

Music: Henry Mancini
Additional Music: Frank Wildhorn
Lyrics: Leslie Bricusse
Book: Blake Edwards
Producer: Tony Adams, Blake Edwards,
Polygram Diversified Entr.
Director: Blake Edwards
Choreographer: Rob Marshall

Song Highlights:
Crazy World; Le Jazz Hot;
Living In The Shadows (Wildhorn);
Paris By Night; Victor/Victoria

Cast:
Julie Andrews, Michael Cripe, Hillel Gitter,
Adam Heller, Gregory Jbara, Michael Nouri,
Tony Roberts, Richard B. Shull, Rachel York

CRAZY WORLD

Lyric by
LESLIE BRICUSSE

Music by
HENRY MANCINI

Crazy World - 5 - 1

Crazy World - 5 - 5

IN WHATEVER TIME WE HAVE

Music and Lyrics by
STEPHEN SCHWARTZ

Flowing, with sincerity and simplicity ♩ = 112

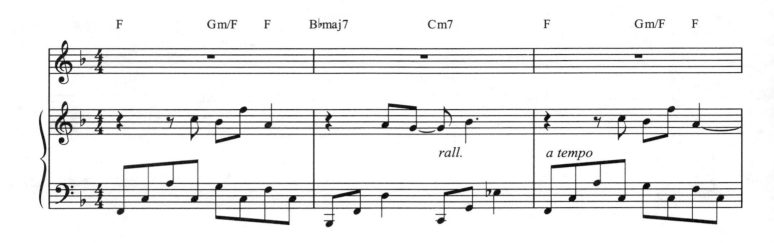

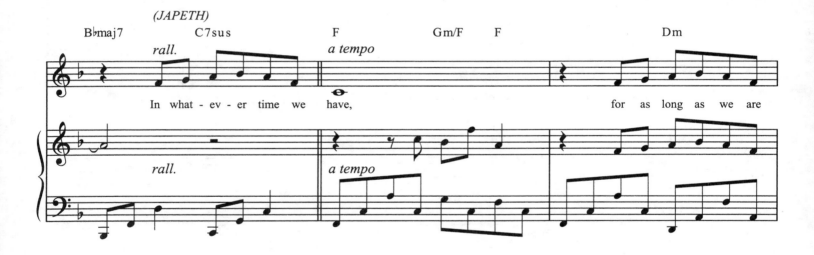

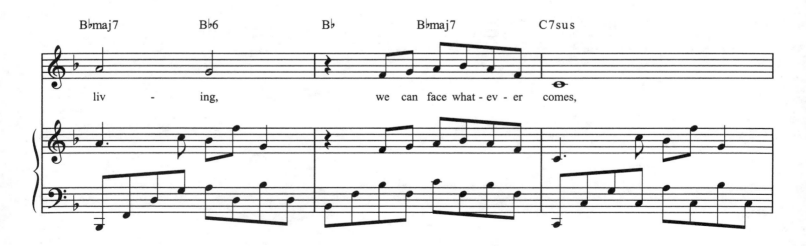

In Whatever Time We Have - 7 - 1

In Whatever Time We Have - 7 - 2

Steel Pier

SECOND CHANCE

Lyrics by
FRED EBB

Music by
JOHN KANDER

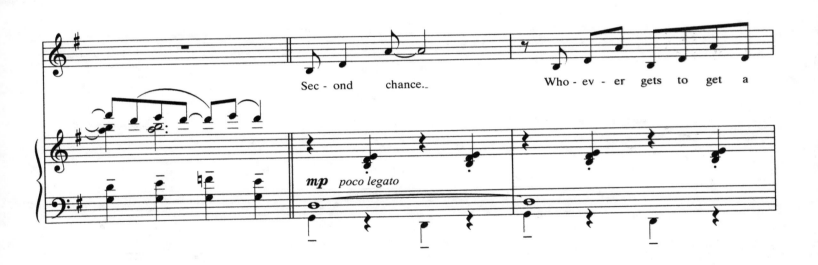

Second Chance - 5 - 1

388

Second Chance - 5 - 2

down, they say._____ Once_____ you're out, you're

out to stay._____ No one tells_____

_____ you you can get right_____ up and you can start all

o - ver with a sec - ond chance.__ When - ev - er life has gone from

f *dim.* *cresc.*

To Coda ⊕

D.S. 𝄋 al Coda

⊕ Coda

A sec - ond chance.

SOMEBODY OLDER

Lyrics by
FRED EBB

Music by
JOHN KANDER

Somebody Older - 4 - 1

394

be some-one a lot like me.

Some-bod-y wis-er who's been a-round_____ Can

Somebody Older - 4 - 3

Somebody Older - 4 - 4

CLOSER THAN EVER

Lyrics by
RICHARD MALTBY, JR.

Music by
DAVID SHIRE

Closer Than Ever - 4 - 1

Closer Than Ever - 4 - 4

Passion

LOVING YOU

Music and Lyrics by
STEPHEN SONDHEIM

Largo tranquillo ♩ = 56

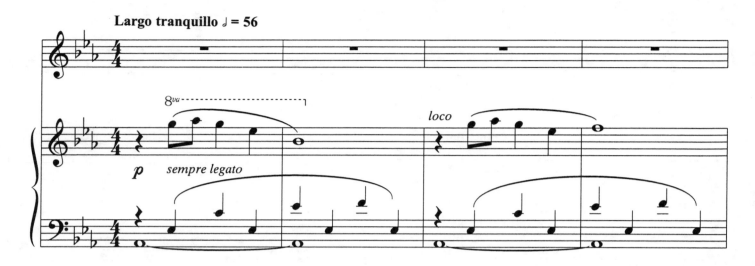

Lov - ing you is not a choice, It's who I am.

Lov - ing you is not a choice, And not much rea - son

Loving You - 3 - 1

Lov - ing you is not in my con - trol. But lov - ing you, I have a goal, for what's left of my life. I will live, And I would die for you.

RAGTIME

Emma Goldman giving one of her fiery speeches

Opened: 01/18/1998
Ford Center for the Performing Arts
Broadway: 834 performances

Music: Stephen Flaherty
Lyrics: Lynn Ahrens
Book: Terrence McNally
Producer: Livent, Inc.
Director: Frank Galati
Choreographer: Graciela Daniele

Song Highlights:
Back To Before; New Music; Ragtime;
Sarah Brown Eyes; 'Til We Reach That Day;
Wheels Of A Dream

Cast:
Jim Corti, Peter Friedman, Tommy Hollis,
Mark Jacoby, Judy Kaye, Marin Mazzie,
Audra McDonald, Brian Stokes Mitchell,
Lynette Perry, Steven Sutcliffe

WHEELS OF A DREAM

Lyrics by
LYNN AHRENS

Music by
STEPHEN FLAHERTY

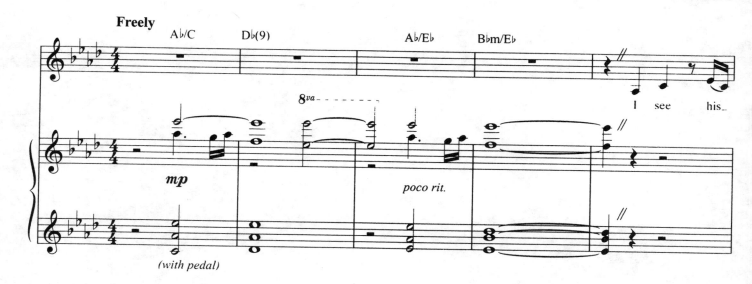

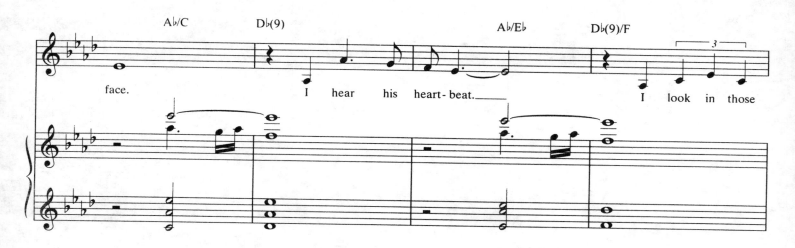

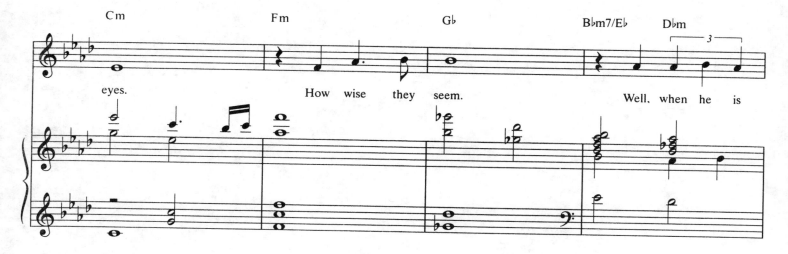

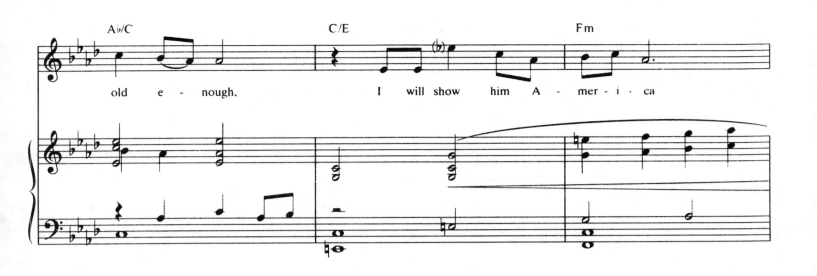

old e-nough, I will show him A-mer-i-ca

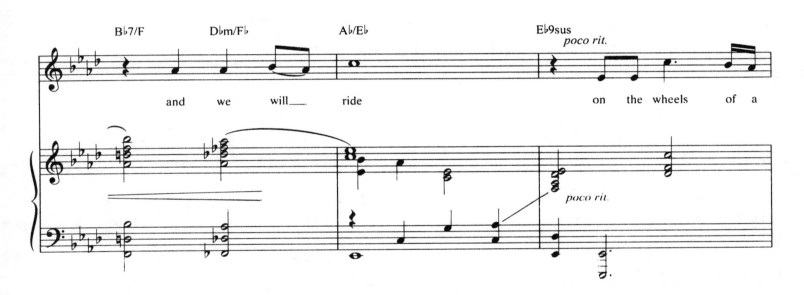

and we will ride on the wheels of a

dream... We'll go down

Coalhouse:

Wheels of a Dream - 10 - 2

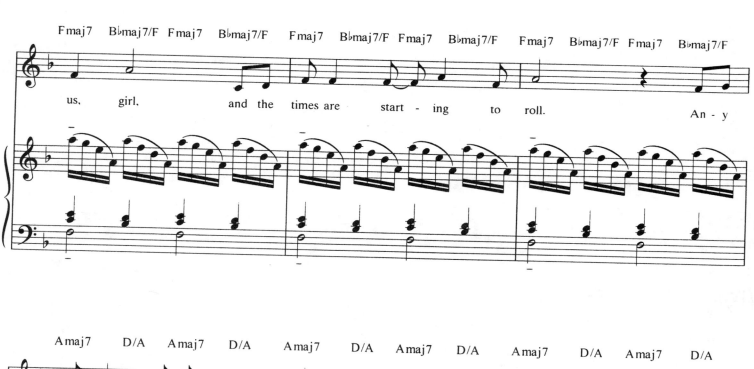

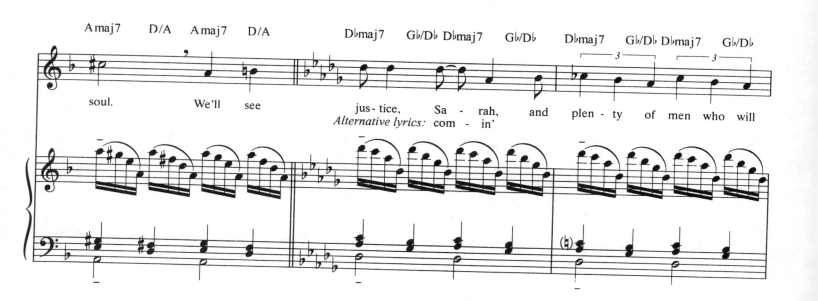

Wheels of a Dream - 10 - 10

Ragtime

MAKE THEM HEAR YOU

Lyrics by
LYNN AHRENS

Music by
STEPHEN FLAHERTY

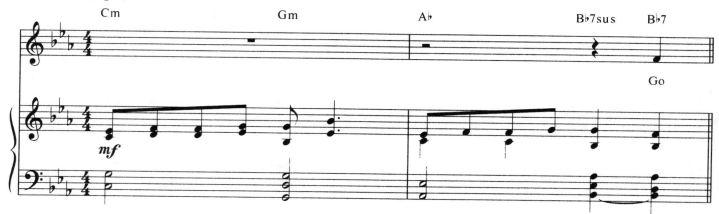

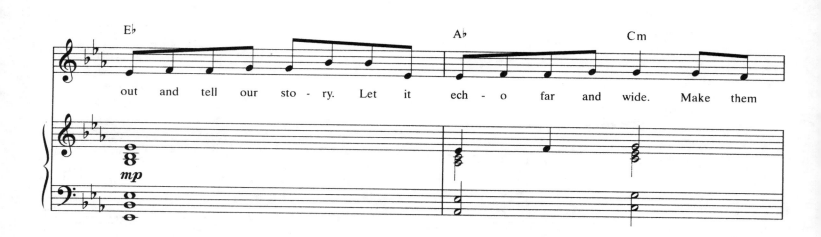

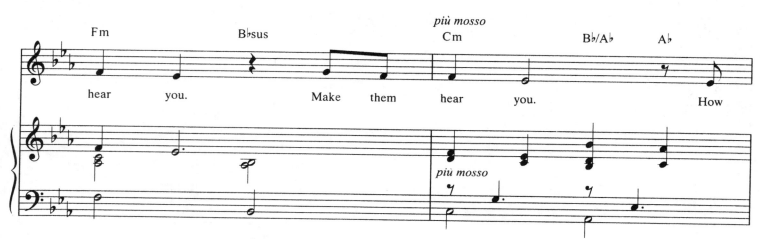

Make Them Hear You - 5 - 1

Make Them Hear You - 5 - 2

Make Them Hear You - 5 - 5

Singin' In The Rain

YOU ARE MY LUCKY STAR

Words by
ARTHUR FREED

Music by
NACIO HERB BROWN

THE SCARLET PIMPERNEL

Terrence Mann and Christine Andreas

Opened: 11/09/1997
The Minskoff Theatre
Broadway: 843 performances

Music: Frank Wildhorn
Lyrics: Nan Knighton
Book: Nan Knighton
Director: Peter Hunt
(Revised production: Robert Longbottom)
Producer: Pierre Cossette, Bill Haber, Hallmark
Entertainment, Ted Forstmann, Kathleen Raitt
Choreographer: Adam Pelty
(Revised production: Robert Longbottom)

Songs Highlights:
The Creation Of Man; Into The Fire; Storyboook;
They Seek Him Here; When I Look At You;
You Are My Home

Cast:
Christine Andreas, Pamela Barrell,
Ed Dixon, Phillip Hoffman, Marine Jahan,
Terrence Mann, Sandy Rosenberg,
Douglas Sills, Gilles Schiasson

The Scarlet Pimpernel

YOU ARE MY HOME

Lyrics by
NAN KNIGHTON

Music by
FRANK WILDHORN

You Are My Home - 4 - 1

The Secret Garden

HOW COULD I EVER KNOW?

Lyrics by
MARSHA NORMAN

Music by
LUCY SIMON

How Could I Ever Know? - 3 - 1

Piano arrangement by Michael Kosarin

MR. BOJANGLES

Words and Music by
JERRY JEFF WALKER

Mr. Bojangles - 2 - 1

FOSSE

Scott Wise (center) and Cast

Opened: 01/14/99
Broadhurst Theatre
Broadway: Still running at press time

Music: Various Composers
Lyrics: Various
Producer: Livent, Inc.
Director: Richard Maltby, Jr.
Choreographer: Bob Fosse (Re-created by Chet Walker)

Song Highlights:
Big Spender; Life Is Just A Bowl Of Cherries;
Mr. Bojangles; Razzle Dazzle;
Sing! Sing! Sing!; Steam Heat

Cast:
Eugene Fleming, Kim Morgan Greene,
Mary Ann Lamb, Jane Lanier, Dana Moore,
Elizabeth Parkinson, Valerie Pettiford,
Desmond Richardson, Sergio Trujillo, Scott Wise